B M W

PERFORMANCE WITH LUXURY

by
SHIRLEY HAINES
and
HARRY HAINES

THE ROURKE CORPORATION, INC.
Vero Beach, FL 32964

CREDITS

The authors and publisher wish to thank BMW of North America for invaluable assistance in compiling the technical information for this book. Special thanks are due Robert Mitchell for locating the photographs, all of which were obtained from BMW. Special appreciation is owed to Bill Cato of the Autoplex (BMW's dealer in Amarillo, Texas) for his continuous help, guidance and encouragement.

Thanks to Ken Parker for the drawing of Germany on page 5.

Library of Congress Cataloging-in-Publication Data

Haines, Shirley, 1935-
    BMW: performance with luxury / by Shirley and
Harry Haines.
        p.   cm. – (Car classics)
    Includes index.
    Summary: Gives a brief history of the BMW automobile
and describes its special features and some classic models.
    ISBN 0-86593-251-4
    1. BMW automobile – History – Juvenile literature.
[1. BMW automobile.] I. Haines, Harry, 1932-   . II. Title.
III. Series: Car classics (Vero Beach, Fla.)
TL215.B43H35   1993
629.222'2 – dc20   92-43260
                                                                    CIP
                                                                    AC
Printed in the USA

CONTENTS

1. "The Best Car in the World" 4

2. The Beginning: Aircraft Engines 6

3. BMW Motorcycles...8

4. BMW's First Automobiles 10

5. Cars in the 1930s 12

6. After World War II 14

7. Cars of the '60s and '70s 16

8. The Kidney Shaped Grill 18

9. Racing 20

10. BMW Today: The 3-Series 22

11. BMW Today: 5-Series and 7-Series 24

12. BMW's Top-of-the-Line 26

13. Future BMW Automobiles 28

14. BMW: Important Dates 30

    Glossary 31

    Index 32

CHAPTER 1

"THE BEST CAR IN THE WORLD"

A person's first impression of BMW is that the initials probably refer to something British. Not surprisingly, recent surveys made by the company show there are still a few people around the world who have not yet learned that the "B" stands for "Bavaria," a region in southern Germany where the company was founded in 1916. The official German name, "Bayerische Motoren Werke," translates as "Bavarian Motor Works."

Whatever uncertainties may exist about the name, there is no misunderstanding about BMW's reputation as an automobile of outstanding quality. Rarely in the history of motor vehicles has any car been so consistently praised by the press. *Car and*

An 850i, BMW's top-of-the-line car for the 1990s. It features a 12-cylinder engine with a 6-speed manual shift. Top speed of the American version is limited by an electronic governor to 155 mph.

Driver magazine calls it, "The Neiman-Marcus of sports sedans." A BMW model has been included on virtually every "Top Ten" list of automobiles in the past quarter century. The readers of *Auto Motor and Sport* voted BMW "The Best Car in the World" for three successive years.

The world headquarters of BMW is housed in this very unusual building located in Munich. Its "four cylinders" have 22 stories and provide offices for 2,000 workers. The world famous BMW Museum is pictured in the foreground with "BMW" on the roof.

BMW is located in Munich, Germany. However, much of the history of its automobiles takes place in Eisenach, and all motorcycles are now made in Berlin.

CHAPTER 2

THE BEGINNING: AIRCRAFT ENGINES

The Bavarian Motor Works was chartered to begin business on March 7, 1916, in the city of Munich, Germany. The new firm was founded to build aircraft engines. Its engines were of outstanding quality, and the new company expanded rapidly to meet the needs of the German Air Force during World War I.

BMW aircraft engines immediately set new records for performance and, as a result, the orders poured in. One large 1918 military contract called for the production of 3,000 aviation engines. In just two years after its founding, the Bavarian Motor Works had become a stock company with a fantastic balance sheet. By October, 1918, BMW had 3,500 employees producing 150 aircraft engines a month. However, the war ended in November, 1918 and the market for aviation engines collapsed. New product lines would have to be developed, or the end of the war would be the beginning of the end for BMW.

A typical World War I German fighter plane powered by a BMW engine.

First design for a BMW emblem (representing a stylized propeller), 1917.

The BMW signet as it appeared in 1929 on the first BMW automobiles.

Today's BMW badge, which was first used in 1963.

Number 4 Wing of Baron von Richthofen's (the Red Baron) pursuit squadron waits to get airborne.

CHAPTER 3

BMW MOTORCYCLES

Following World War I, the future looked bleak for BMW. A worldwide reputation as a designer-builder of record breaking airplane motors was of little value. The company searched desperately for a new market and tried a number of alternatives. One of their most successful efforts was the building of small engines for motorcycles. By 1921 BMW had developed a 6.5 horsepower (hp) engine called the "Bayern Klein Motor" (Bavarian Small Engine). Designated the M1B15, this little 2-cylinder powerplant was an engineering marvel and sold well to motorcycle manufacturers all over Europe.

The next step seemed obvious: BMW should build the "whole" motorcycle, not just the engine.

The K1, one of the most aerodynamically correct motorcycles ever produced. Wind-tunnel-tested to provide the rider with an envelope of calm air, it is the epitome of the modern sports-touring motorcycle.

This rare photo shows the manufacturing plant of the 1920s with BMW's first great motorcycle, the R32. It was known for its reliability and top speed of 60 mph.

Ernst Henne set 21 world speed records in the 1930s with BMW motorcycles. This fully faired-in streamliner is representative of a number of machines that he used. His record of 173 mph on the Darmstadt Autobahn lasted until the 1950s.

Their first, the BMW R32, was produced in late fall, 1923. It broke new ground with its driveshaft to the rear wheel and is now regarded as one of the most ingenious design developments in the history of the motorcycle. The R32 and the models that followed sold well and saved the company. By 1929 BMW made the fastest motorcycles in the world.

Motorcycles were especially popular in the hard times of the '20s and '30s. BMW machines became famous for their engineering quality and speed. This tradition has continued through the years and is, more than ever, true today. Since the 1960s, all BMW motorcycles have been produced in Berlin. The little M1B15 engine (in a modern, improved version) is still being made today.

CHAPTER 4

BMW'S FIRST AUTOMOBILES

Twice a manufacturing success by the late 1920s, BMW could see that the future was not in aircraft engines nor motorcycles … it was in automobiles. The quickest way to get into the business was to buy one; the Dixi plant in nearby Eisenach was for sale. In the fall of 1928 BMW took over.

Dixi (Latin for "I have spoken") cars were among the smallest cars produced in the late 1920s. From today's viewpoint, they looked cute, tiny, even funky. However, when the Great Depression hit in October, 1929, and continued into the 1930s, it was an advantage to be in the small car end of the automotive business.

BMW's sales depended on expansion of its dealer network. Many of its motorcycle dealers added cars to their business. In some German cities

A 1932 20 hp BMW. In answer to the question, "Who bought BMWs in the early 1930s?" BMW's magazine, Blätter, declared in its June, 1930 issue, "It is the Woman! BMW believes that it has met the lady's requirements with this 0.75 liter car. It can be steered by the most tender hand."

Model	BMW 3/20
Period of production	1932-34
Number of cylinders	4
Horsepower @ rpm	20 @ 3500
Gearbox	3-speed; after July, 1933, 4-speed
Maximum speed	50 mph
Units produced	7,215

one could even buy a new BMW at the friendly Mercedes dealer. The little BMW was a welcome addition to a dealer where the cheapest Mercedes was priced at 6,000 marks — almost two-and-a-half times what the little BMW cost.

A Dixi 3/15 of the late 1920s. The "3" referred to taxable horsepower and the "15" was the maximum engine horsepower.

The Dixi 3/15 was made under license of the Austin Automobile Company of England. It was almost identical to the "Austin 7" of the late 1920s.

CHAPTER 5

CARS IN THE 1930s

In 1933, at the peak of the Great Depression, BMW was the fifth largest German auto maker after Opel, Auto Union, Mercedes and Adler. Fifth place was a 5.8 percent market share with 5,832 vehicles produced, up from 5.4 percent the previous year. BMW's mildly positive sales trend was due to two factors: (1) increasing demand for the little 3/20 cars, and (2) a new model which was to forecast BMW's future. The new model 303 appeared at the Frankfurt Auto Show in February, 1933; it was the first BMW to display the now traditional "kidney" radiator grill. The model 303 quickly became the 326 and was the most successful BMW of the 1930s. Subsequent variations were labeled the 327, 320 and 321. The 320 was built until the end of 1938 and then replaced by the 321.

For BMW devotees, *the* car of the decade was the 328. It made a spectacular first appearance on June 14, 1936 by entering and winning the race at Nürburgring against the best supercharged sports cars of the day. Its

A 1934 BMW 315. The 315 was the successor to the 303. Like other models of this early 3-series, its chassis was lubricated by a one-shot system, operated by the driver with a foot pedal at "suggested" 30-mile intervals.

Model	315	328
Period of production	1934-37	1936-40
Number of cylinders	6	6
Horsepower @ rpm	34 @ 4000	80 @ 5000
Gearbox	4-speed	4-speed
Maximum speed	62 mph	93 mph
Units produced	9,521	461

A BMW 337 coupe, probably a 1937 model (it was made from 1937 to 1941). Considered a classic by today's vintage authorities, it was essentially a sporty version of the 326 and used the same chassis and powerplant.

average speed was 62.9 mph. The new two-seater didn't look like a race car, just a handsome roadster. In style, it ushered in a new era: headlights in the fenders, only a hint of running boards left, streamlined body, no outside door handles, and its two leather straps across the hood recalled the classical sports car. The 328 set new standards for engineering with a new suspension system, hydraulic shocks and hydraulic brakes. The most remarkable feature of the new car, however, was its engine. The numbers were the best and set the standard for the era.

The BMW 328 sport. One of the most attractive sports cars of the '30s and a big winner in competitions. Because of the war in the '40s, its racing career extended well into the '50s. Today it is the most sought-after classic BMW.

CHAPTER 6

AFTER WORLD WAR II

A BMW 502 Limousine. The ultimate Baroque Angel or '50s luxury car. Most were produced in only one color, black, and did not sell well. However, they kept the name BMW alive as an automobile of high quality.

V-E Day in 1945 left most of Germany in ruins and no business was harder hit than BMW. Starting with less than a thousand workers, the company lived from hand to mouth, scraping a fragile existence producing a few bicycles, aluminum baking utensils and agricultural machinery. Older workers who remembered times after WW I must have smiled when BMW accepted an order to produce railway brake sets.

The model R50. A post-World War II motorcycle with swing-arm suspension that made the BMW one of the most comfortable road bikes of the day.

Model	501/502 V-8	Isetta
Period of production	1954-61	1955-62
Number of cylinders	8	1
Horsepower @ rpm	100 @ 4800	12 @ 5800
Transmission	4-speed	4-speed
Maximum speed	99 mph	53 mph
Units produced	5,955	161,728

Motorcycles became the first post-war success. In 1948 production began, and by 1950 over 7,000 units had been sold. In that year, BMW employed over 8,700 people and even managed to make a small profit. Plans were made to again begin building automobiles. The engineers knew what they wanted to make, but BMW had no drawings, few tools, and raw material prices were sky high. However, the biggest hurdle was political. Unlike Mercedes, Opel and Volkswagen, BMW had no plant to rebuild. The company's prewar cars had all been built in Eisenach, which was across the line in East Germany.

Forced to start fresh in Munich with new designs *and* a new plant, BMW entered the '50s with two approaches: (1) a series of luxury cars nicknamed the "Baroque Angels" after the voluptuous, rather fleshy ladies found in so many Bavarian churches, and (2) the Isetta, an Italian designed economy car known as the "bubble car."

The "bubble car," the Isetta. It had only one door on the front, held two people, got 43 miles per gallon, and reached a top speed of 53 mph. It was powered by an air-cooled 12 hp engine taken from the R25 motorcycle. Between 1955 and 1962, BMW sold an amazing 161,728 of these tiny cars. Later models added a back seat and a side door. With a larger engine, the model 600 reached a top speed of 62 mph.

CHAPTER 7

CARS OF THE '60s AND '70s

First of the "new class" of BMWs, the model 1500 was produced in the years 1962-64. It became the forerunner of an entire dynasty of BMW automobiles.

The Frankfurt International Auto Show of 1961 was BMW's turning point. The new 1500 model was introduced to rave reviews. Its good proportions, its lively turn of speed, and its exemplary handling established the company once and for all as worthy of "world-class" recognition. In the years 1962-64, some 23,807 copies of this model were produced, a new record for BMW.

Next came the 1800 with a bigger engine, then the 1600 with better engineering detail. These were followed by a number of models and constant improvements. Especially notable were the 2000 and the 2002, the latter accounting for 339,084 units produced between 1968-1976. Demand for BMW cars had taken on such proportions by 1968-69 that German customers were waiting as long as nine months for delivery of a new car.

Model	1500	2000 CS	2002
Period of production	1962-64	1965-69	1968-76
Number of cylinders	4	4	4
Horsepower @ rpm	80 @ 5700	120 @ 5500	100 @ 5500
Transmission	4-speed manual	4-speed manual	4-speed manual or 3-speed automatic
Maximum speed	92 mph	115 mph	107 mph
Units produced	23,807	8,883	339,084

The 2002, a large smooth engine in a compact car. Introduced in 1968, it set the pattern for the range of cars that became the 3-series.

These cars also marked the beginning of significant sales in the United States and established the BMW automobile as a major import. Sales have grown steadily, and today America is the company's largest foreign market.

The 2000 CS (1965-69). If the 1500 began the "new class," the 2000 series confirmed it. The 120 hp engine came with a 4-speed manual transmission and road handling characteristics that were a dream.

CHAPTER 8

THE KIDNEY SHAPED GRILL

How can you tell the "marque" (car manufacturer)? Sometimes it is difficult. We have all seen people walk around an unfamiliar car, looking for its brand name, trying to find out "what kind of car it is."

There are a few cars that have such well-known styling tradition (usually the radiator grill) that their models can be instantly recognized. Two that come immediately to mind are Rolls-Royce and Mercedes. However, no "marque" can top BMW's Kidney Shaped Grill as a design feature for instant recognition. It shouts out to the world the car's heritage, its pedigree.

The twin "Kidneys" seem to have just the right amount of subtlety to carry the car's mystique. Whether it is a sporty little 318i coupe or a big 750iL sedan, those two little openings on the front say, "This car is a BMW and that means quality."

The El Spider, a study for a car of the 21st century. The "Kidney Shaped Grill" confirms its BMW bloodline.

The "Kidney Shaped Grill" as seen on seven generations of BMW coupes from the 1930s to the 1990s. Right to left are as follows: 327 (1937-41), 503 (1956-59), 3200 CS (1962-65), 2000 CS (1965-69), 3 liter CS (1968-75), 635 CSi (1976-89), and in the foreground the 850i, BMW's coupe for the 21st century.

CHAPTER 9

RACING

BMW's first big victory in motor sports was its team prize in the International Alpine Trials of 1929 – the first year of BMW automobiles. The next year brought more victories. Amazingly, the cars that were winning these races were the hardy little 3/15 models with only 15 horsepower.

The car that "will live in history" as the best racer of its era was the BMW 328. After its debut in 1936, it went on to win virtually every race it entered in the 1930s. The best drivers clamored to drive it, and its list of victories established BMW as a leader in automobile engineering and technology.

Following World War II, privately built racing cars with BMW components were frequently visible in the winner's circle. In the 1960s BMW cars were once again competing (and winning) in major races all over the world. In 1972 the company established a racing division called "BMW Motorsport." Bavarian Motor Works was now a major entry (and frequent winner) at places like Riverside, Daytona, Watkins Glen, Mid-Ohio, Laguna Seca and Lime Rock.

Nelson Piquet won three Grand Prix in the Brabham/BMW BT52, as well as the Formula One World Championship.

The Group A M3 in action in 1991. BMW invented the sports sedan, and every car in its lineup reflects this dual quality of racing car spirit with street car looks.

The history of BMW has roughly paralleled the world's record books in aviation, motorcycles and autos. The company has always seemed to attract competitive people, and its engineering leadership has been characterized by competition recognition.

CHAPTER 10

BMW TODAY: THE 3-SERIES

A 1994 325i convertible. Rich Ceppos writing in Car and Driver *magazine says, "The 325i looks good in photos, but not half as stylish as it does in person."*

In the 1990s BMW's 3-series offers two basic choices, the 325i and the 318i. These two cars are the same, just different engines. *Car and Driver* magazine writes about the 325 as follows:

The overriding impression is quality – the savory hum of the machinery, the smooth-as-silk feel of the major controls, the sensory rewards of sure-footed handling. The 325i is motivated by the same twin-cam 24-valve 2.5 liter in-line six as the larger 525i sedan – and we do mean motivated. The engine makes an impressive 189 hp at 5900 rpm. It's a perky motor, the kind you associate more often with sports cars, with maximum torque occurring at 4700 rpm – higher in the rev range than many engines' horsepower peaks. Which is to say, when you want to go, you have to have about 4000 rpm on the clock. Keep the revs up and the 325i is a rocket; it takes only 6.9 seconds to get to 60 mph and 16.3 seconds to cover the quarter-mile, at which point you are hauling buns to the tune of 91 mph. Not long ago we raved about muscle cars that could go that fast.

Racing car technology is also at work in the 1.8 liter, 16-valve, 4-cylinder engine in the 318i. This high

*A 1992 318i coupe.
Remarkably, the engine
requires no valve or timing
adjustments during regular
service checks. That's
because every second it's
running, it is making
adjustments to itself.
BMW's advanced motronics
have eliminated the need for
a distributor altogether.*

performance engine produces 138 horsepower at
6000 rpm and develops 129 pound feet (lb-ft) of
torque at 4500 rpm.

Auto Week Magazine says, "The BMW (3-series)
is the standard against which all sports sedans are
judged." Both the 318i and the 325i are available at
several luxury levels as coupes, sedans, convertibles
and station wagons. Obviously, the 3-series is
BMW's biggest seller.

After several years of research, BMW
announced in June, 1992 that it will invest about
$300 million to build a plant in Greer, South
Carolina. The state-of-the-art factory will be capable
of producing about 70,000 cars a year and is
scheduled to open in 1995. The "US-made" BMW
will be a derivative of the current 3-series.

Model	318i	325i
Number of cylinders	4	6
Horsepower @ rpm (SAE)	138 @ 6000	189 @ 5900
Transmission	4-speed manual or automatic	4-speed manual or automatic
Acceleration		
0-50 mph (sec.)	7.1	5.6
0-60 mph	9.9	7.8
1/4 mile	17.4	15.8
Top speed (limited electronically)	128 mph	128 mph

CHAPTER 11

BMW TODAY: 5-SERIES AND 7-SERIES

BMW's largest and most luxurious cars, the 7-series, are offered in two engine options: the big 4.0 liter V-8, and the huge 5.0 liter V-12. The two body styles are big and bigger, with an "L" designating the longer of the two.

The 5-series, BMW's mid-size auto, comes with two basic engines, a 6-cylinder with 24 valves, and a V-8 with 32 valves. The 2.5 liter is the same engine used in the popular 3-series cars, and the larger 4.0 liter V-8 is the same one used in the big cars, the 7-series. BMW is firm on a long-held position: 6-cylinders in-line is one of the smoothest engine configurations available, and considerably smoother than a V-6. With four valves per cylinder and roof-shaped combustion chamber, optimum combustion is ensured and the result is an engine of high efficiency.

Automobile Magazine quotes Robert Buchelhofer, the BMW board member in charge of sales: "Spending money to buy image, which was

When speaking BMW, "Touring" means station wagon. Pictured here is a 1992 525i Touring. Georg Kacher, writing in the November, 1992 Automobile Magazine, *says, "The four-door 525i Touring is still the car to beat when it comes to handling and roadholding."*

A '93 model 525i. The numbering system tells that it is a "5-series" with a "2.5 liter" engine. The sound of smoothness, so unique that it unlike any other car, tells that it is BMW.

part of the Eighties, maybe – that's over. Price, value, and image have to be combined." BMW is certainly trying to do that with their 5- and 7-series. These cars offer a combination of form and function that is a design "tour de force" which sets them apart from anything else on the road.

The biggest BMW, the 750iL. This big car with its 12-cylinder engine is elegance and performance taken to the highest level. The 7-series has been called "the very definition of understated elegance."

Model	525i	540i	750iL
Number of cylinders	6	8	V-12
Horsepower @ rpm (SAE)	189 @ 5900	282 @ 5800	296 @ 5200
Transmission	5-speed manual or 4-speed automatic	5-speed automatic	4-speed automatic
Acceleration			
0-50 mph (sec.)	6.3	5.2	5.5
0-60 mph	8.6	6.7	7.1
1/4 mile	16.5	15.1	15.4
Top speed (limited electronically)	128 mph	149 mph	155 mph

27.956

CHAPTER 12

BMW'S TOP-OF-THE-LINE

Only a V-12 engine would do for BMW's top-of-the-line car.

As expected, BMW's 850i comes with the best of everything.

The engine is Germany's most successful 12-cylinder in the last 50 years. It was designed from a "no compromises" philosophy ... no doubling-up of the already-in-production 6-cylinder. The result is one of the lightest 12-cylinders ever built, a 5 liter engine that develops 296 hp and has a maximum torque of 332 lb-ft at 4100 rpm. All engine functions are controlled by BMW's sophisticated Digital Motor Electronics (DME), whose sensors precisely monitor and control all engine functions at their optimum levels.

The 850i is also noted for its innovative suspension design. Officially, it's called a double-pivot spring strut suspension. It uses coil spring/shock absorber units (struts), lower wishbones, an anti-roll bar and hydraulically dampened control links. The track, the distance between wheels from left to right, is an inch wider than on the big 750iL luxury sedan! The resulting advantages of all this are stable straight-line running, minimal dive under braking, low transmission levels of road noise, and tremendous cornering ability.

The 850i is visible proof that luxury is more than exquisite leather, thick carpeting, wood paneling and a long list of "options" that come as standard features. As their slogan says, "It is the ultimate in driving satisfaction."

Left: The pinnacle of BMW automotive design is this 12-cylinder coupe, the 850i. More than any other car, it proves that elegance and performance are not mutually exclusive.

A 6-speed manual transmission, the first on any series production car and the only one available with a V-12 engine today, is standard on the 850i.

Model	850i
Number of cylinders	V-12
Capacity (cubic inches)	304.4
Horsepower @ rpm (SAE)	296 @ 5200
Transmission	6-speed manual
Acceleration	
0-60 mph	6.1
1/4 mile	14.7
Top speed (limited electronically)	155 mph

CHAPTER 13

FUTURE BMW AUTOMOBILES

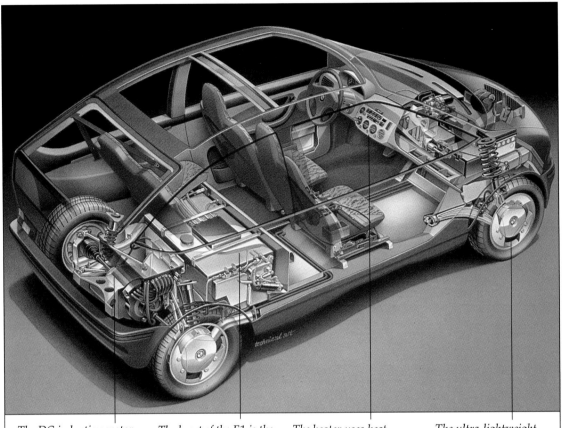

The DC induction motor with integral differential has a maximum rating of 45 hp. It is mounted centrally on the rear axle.

The heart of the E1 is the 120 volt sodium sulphur battery. Recharging takes between six and eight hours.

The heater uses heat dissipated by the electric motor and battery and is absolutely pollutant-free.

The ultra-lightweight wheels, with their integrated brake drums, come with BMW's standard ABS.

Quietly, the future draws nearer.

The E1 electric automobile is more than just a technical exercise or design study. It is the way of the future. The E1's technical features have been planned down to the smallest detail and matched to people's needs. The windshield, for instance, is slanted steeply to lower the drag and therefore has a coating to reflect infrared rays and reduce overheating in strong sunlight.

The E1's operating radius is, at present, an impressive 150 miles. Normal recharging is six to eight hours, but a rapid charger is available that requires less than two hours. Readers of *Auto Zeitung* magazine voted the E1 the "Best Study for the Automobile of the Future."

Model	BMW E1	BMW E2
Weight (in kilograms)	880	915
Drag coefficient	.32	.32
Maximum power output (kW)	32	32
Battery capacity (kWh)	19.2	28.8
Acceleration 0-50 km/h	6 seconds	N.A.
0/80 km/h	18 seconds	N.A.
Top speed	120 km/h	120 km/h

The E1 has now been joined by the E2, a second prototype designed for the American market. Weighing about 2,205 pounds, 220 pounds heavier than the E1, the E2 delivers even more impressive performance. Powered by an electric motor producing approximately 43 hp, the E2 is anticipated to accelerate to 31 mph in 6.5 seconds and to 50 mph in 15.6 seconds. It is estimated to reach a top speed of 75 mph, and its typical range under normal driving conditions should be 161 miles.

The BMW E1, the company's prototype for the electric car of the future. Auto Bild *says: "Right now, the E1 is this century's most modern car."*

The E2. BMW's second generation electric car was designed to meet California's low emissions law, which requires 1 percent of all automobiles sold in 1998 to be electric-powered. This will rise to 5 percent in 2001 and to 10 percent in 2003.

CHAPTER 14

BMW: IMPORTANT DATES

1916 BMW is chartered to do business in Munich, Germany. The company's only product is an aircraft engine.

1919 A BMW engine mounted in a World War I biplane reaches 32,000 feet, a world altitude record.

1923 BMW's first motorcycle, the R32, appears on the market. With a Boxer engine and shaft drive, it becomes a leader in the motorcycle industry.

1928 BMW takes over the Dixi Automobile Company in Eisenach, Germany.

1929 The first production BMW cars are made. Called the 3/15, they are tiny, cute little cars with a .75 liter engine rated at a maximum of 15 horsepower.

1933 The first BMW designed auto, the 303, is introduced. It has the Kidney Shaped Grill that will be featured on all future cars.

1936 The new model 328 creates a sensation at Nürburgring. It is the fastest production road car of its day.

1939 Germany attacks Poland and World War II stops all automobile manufacturing. BMW turns to motorcycles and aircraft engines.

1945 V-E Day finds BMW in ruins. Worse yet, the automobile factory in Eisenach is located in East Germany and is taken over by the Communist Government.

1947 BMW struggles to survive by manufacturing pots and pans, train brakes and motorcycles. There are 1,000 employees.

1949 The motorcycle market flourishes. BMW employees increase to 3,000 and the company announces a small profit.

1951 The first post-war car is introduced. It is a model 501 shown at the Frankfurt Auto Show.

1952 The BMW 501 begins production. A total of 50 cars are manufactured that year.

1955 The Isetta begins production. A total of 161,728 "bubble cars" are produced through 1962.

1961 The turning point for the company, the 1500 debuts at the Frankfurt Auto Show.

1965 The debut of the 2000 CS. Between 1968-1976, BMW sells 339,084 of the model 2002.

1969 BMW introduces a new line of completely redesigned motorcycles.

1972 A new range of models is introduced beginning with the 520. The first 6-cylinder model of this new series appears a year later as the BMW 525.

1975 The first 3-series appears on the market in July. These new sports sedans have a completely new body design.

1978 BMW becomes the first German manufacturer to equip an automobile – the BMW 528i – with a controlled 3-way catalytic converter.

1983 Nelson Piquet makes BMW the first turbo Formula 1 world champion in the history of motor sport. The 800 hp, 1.5 liter BMW engine in the Brabham BT52 beat all competition.

1986 The 7-series bring new standards of size and luxury to the BMW lineup.

1988 BMW re-introduces the V-12 engine.

1990 The 850i sports coupe sets a new standard that redefines the company's slogan, "the ultimate driving machine."

1991 BMW's electric car, the E1, is introduced. Plans are announced for the E2.

1992 For the first time in history, BMW sells more cars than its chief rival, Mercedes.

GLOSSARY

Bavaria – A region located in the southeast part of Germany.

Bayerische – German spelling for Bavarian.

chassis – The basic frame of the vehicle, on which all other parts are mounted.

driveshaft – The mechanical link from the engine to the wheel(s) that move the vehicle.

Kidney Shaped Grill – A twin (at first round, then almost square) opening on the front of all BMW cars from 1933 to the present, which has become their design trademark.

km/h – Kilometers per hour. The speed of a car.

limousine – A large luxurious car, often driven by a chauffeur.

marque – Trademark. Especially the name by which cars of a certain manufacturer are most widely known.

motronics – BMW's name for the electrical system that supplies the engine's ignition.

mph – Miles per hour. The speed of a car.

Munich – The capital and largest city of Bavaria.

mystique – An aura of mystery or mystical power. In cars, that indefinable quality which adds to its image and increases its desirablility.

SAE – Society of Automotive Engineers. The acronym most often used today to indicate a standard way of calculating the horsepower of an automobile.

INDEX

Aircraft engines 6, 10
Airplane, World War I 6, 8
Austin Automobile Company 11
Auto Motor and Sport 5
Auto Week Magazine 23
Auto Zeitung Magazine 28
Automobile Magazine 24
Bavaria 4
Bavarian Motor Works 4, 6, 20
Berlin, Germany 5
Blätter 10
BMW cars
    3 liter CS 19
    3-series 22, 23
    5-series 24, 25
    7-series 24, 25
    303 12
    315 12
    318i 18, 22, 23
    325i 22, 23
    326 12, 13
    327 12, 18
    328 12, 13, 18, 20
    337 13
    502 limousine (Baroque Angel) 14, 15
    503 19
    525i Touring 24, 25
    635 CSi 19
    750iL 18, 25, 27
    850i 4, 19, 26, 27
    1500 16, 17
    1600 16
    1800 16
    2000 16, 17
    2000 CS 16, 17, 19
    2002 16, 17
    3200 CS 19
    E1 electric auto 28, 29
    E2 electric auto 28, 29
    El Spider 18
    Isetta 15
BMW emblem 7
BMW Motorsport 20
BMW Museum 5
Brabham/BMW BT52 20

Car and Driver 4, 5, 22
Dixi car 10, 11
Eisenach, Germany 5, 10, 15
El Spider (car) 18
Henne, Ernst 9
International Alpine Trials 20
K1 Motorcycle 8
Kidney Shaped Grill 18, 19
M1B15 Motorcycle Engine 8, 9
Mercedes 11, 12, 15, 18
Motorcycles 5, 8, 9, 10, 15, 18
Munich, Germany 5, 6, 15
Nürburgring Race 12
Piquet, Nelson 20
R32 Motorcycle 9
R50 Motorcycle 14
Radiator grill 18
Red Baron 7
6-speed manual transmission 27
12-cylinder engine 4, 25, 27